Animals Uncovered

The inside view of living creatures

By Steve Parker

An Hachette UK Company
www.hachette.co.uk

First published in the USA in 2015 by Ticktock,
an imprint of Octopus Publishing Group Ltd
Carmelite House
50 Victoria Embankment
London, EC4Y 0DZ
www.octopusbooksusa.com
www.ticktockbooks.com

Distributed in the U.S. by
Hachette Book Group USA
1290 Avenue of the Americas
4th and 5th Floors
New York, NY 10020

Distributed in Canada by
Canadian Manda Group
664 Annette Street
Toronto, Ontario,
Canada M6S 2C8

ISBN 978-1-78325-243-5
Printed and bound in China
10 9 8 7 6 5 4 3 2 1

Series Editor: Anna Bowles
Managing Editor: Karen Rigden
Designer: Dan Newman/Perfect Bound Ltd
Creative Director: Miranda Snow
Production Controller: Meskerem Berhane

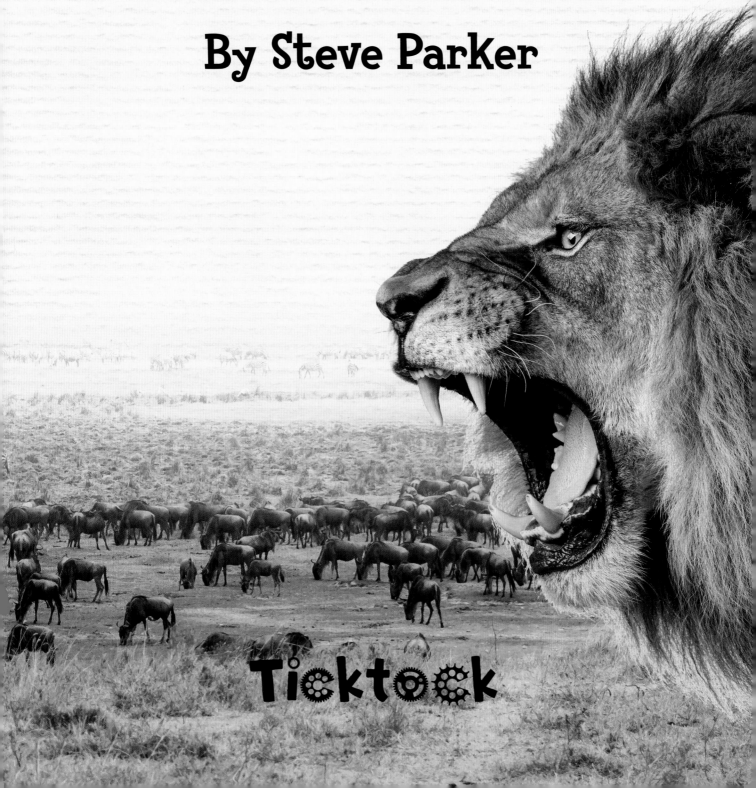

Animals Uncovered

The inside view of living creatures

By Steve Parker

Ticktock

Contents

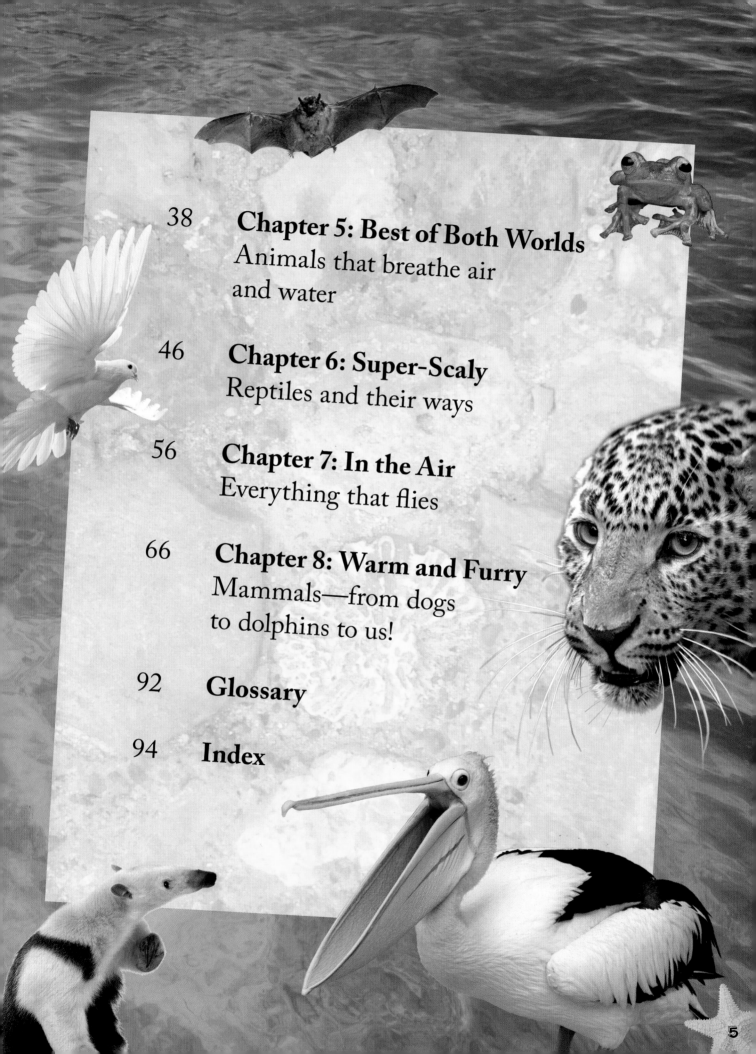

Animals everywhere!

Our world is alive with different animals, from tiny bugs and worms to flying fish, swimming birds, and huge mammals like elephants and whales. Yet they are all surprisingly similar in many ways. All animals need to find food, breathe, sense their surroundings, move about, and escape danger. How? Let's find out...

Animals that eat mostly plants are called **herbivores**. Usually they take in and *digest* a lot because their food is low in nutrients and goodness.

Animals who eat mainly other creatures are **carnivores**. Most are speedy and clever, with fearsome weapons like teeth and claws.

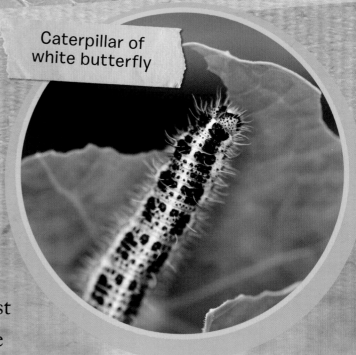

Caterpillar of white butterfly

African wild dog pack

Some animals eat almost any kinds of food including plants and animals. They are known as **omnivores**.

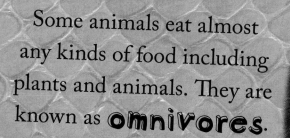

Raccoons eat anything they can get their paws on!

Plants are not animals. They do not eat food, as they make their own food from the light energy found in sunshine.

Habitats

Each kind of animal is suited to certain surroundings, called its *habitat*. Penguins prefer cold seas and icebergs, while parrots like sunny tropical forests. They would not last long in each other's habitat!

Hello, I'm Nosy and my habitat is grasslands. I'm an anteater—but I like termites too!

I'm freezing my feathers off!

Let's take a closer look

All animals, even the tiniest creatures, are full of even tinier parts called **organs** which keep their bodies working. Each organ has an important job to keep the animal alive.

The largest inner parts belong to the biggest animal—the **whale**. Its tongue is the size of a car!

Muscles pull bones to swim and feed

Skeleton of bones supports softer parts

Stomach stores and digests food

Intestines take in nutrients from food

I have a long tongue which helps me taste yummy food!

Animals need to take in **food** for energy to move and *nutrients* to grow. The shark uses its teeth to catch and cut up food for swallowing.

Animals must take in **oxygen**, a substance that is vital for life. Fish have *gills* to take in oxygen from water, as on this goldfish. Many land animals breathe using lungs to get oxygen from air.

Animals **sense** their surroundings in many ways. The leopard has eyes, ears, nose, tongue, and whiskers and skin for touch.

Chapter 1: Single and Simple
The tiniest of the tiny

Some animals are so tiny that as many as 100 could fit into this "o." Yet even creatures this small have organs inside them to do various jobs. Bigger animals do not usually have more organs, just larger ones.

Milions of micro-creatures can be found in half a mugful of pond water.

Any damp or wet place teems with tiny creatures visible only under a microscope. Most are just one living unit, called a **cell**. Yet it does all the vital tasks for life. Some of these micro-living things can also catch energy in sunlight. So they are both animal and plant!

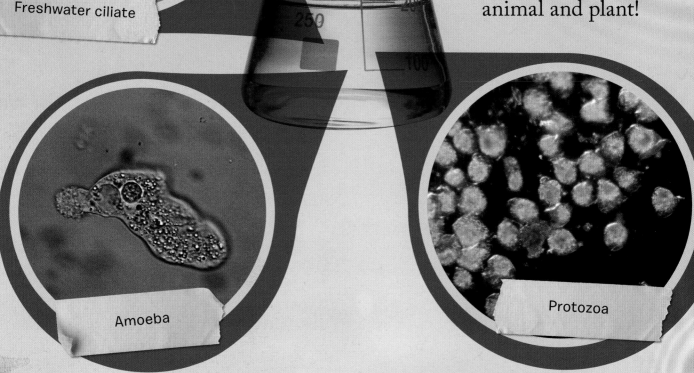

Freshwater ciliate

250

250

100

Amoeba

Protozoa

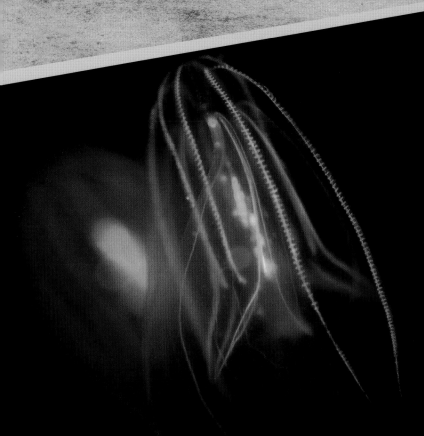

Bigger animals are made up of millions of microscopic cells, specialized in performing different jobs. In the sea, there are simple yet beautiful creatures with thousands of cells, such as sponges, jellyfish, sea anemones, and this **comb jelly.** The micro-hairs on the comb jelly move and wave to propel it through the water.

Some starfish have 12,000 feet. Four is enough for me!

Ring canal

Arm canal

Tube feet (underneath)

Animals have endless ways of getting around. **Starfish** move by an amazing system of thousands of tiny tube feet, pumping water in and out of them from a set of inner pipes called canals.

Simple senses

Even small, simple animals want to find out about the world. Some have no eyes or ears, and can only detect things using touch or smell.

Sponges are the simplest animals. They have no *brain, muscles, nerves, heart, or blood.* But they can sense using touch and they can take in food, which makes them animals.

The **giant clam** has eyespots around its *shell* edge. Clams cannot see in detail; they can only detect light and dark. If it suddenly goes dark, that could mean danger, so the clam snaps its shell shut.

Simply **huge**

Not all simple animals are small. Some jellyfish grow to 6 ft. 6 in. across with *tentacles* 98 ft. 5 in. long!

The **sea cucumber** is a cousin of the starfish. It has no obvious head with senses, although it has a mouth at one end. But its skin detects heat, cold, pressure, and many chemical substances.

My favorite smell is the lovely whiff of a big termites' nest.

Simply food

Even the simplest creatures take in food and break it down into smaller pieces. This process is called digestion and it is needed for energy, growth, and for mending worn-out parts. Many creatures have mouths like us for eating, but some simply soak up the food around them!

Sea anemones look harmless—but they are deadly killers. Their tentacles have powerful stings that they use to catch fish, prawns, and similar prey. A sea anemone's mouth leads into the stomach in the stalk. Later, leftover food wastes come out the same way!

Leftover waste must leave a nasty taste!

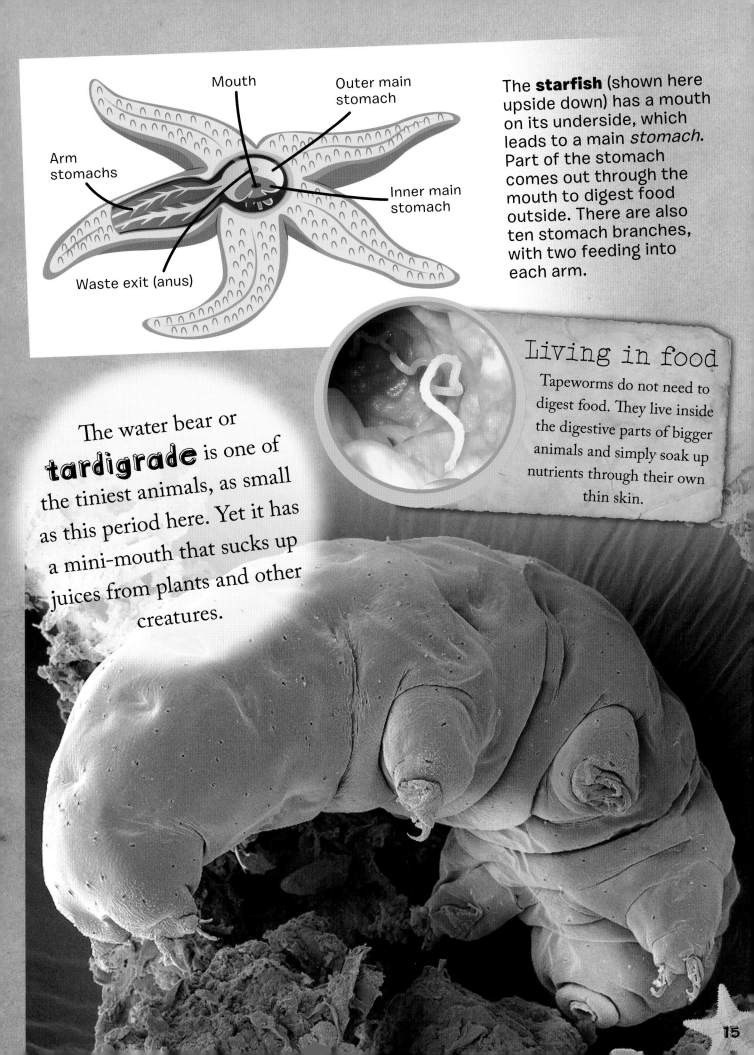

Mouth

Outer main stomach

Arm stomachs

Inner main stomach

Waste exit (anus)

The **starfish** (shown here upside down) has a mouth on its underside, which leads to a main *stomach*. Part of the stomach comes out through the mouth to digest food outside. There are also ten stomach branches, with two feeding into each arm.

Living in food

Tapeworms do not need to digest food. They live inside the digestive parts of bigger animals and simply soak up nutrients through their own thin skin.

The water bear or **tardigrade** is one of the tiniest animals, as small as this period here. Yet it has a mini-mouth that sucks up juices from plants and other creatures.

Chapter 2: Slithery and Slimy
Boneless bodies

Some animals are soft and squishy, with no *bones* inside or shells outside. Worms have long, thin, wriggly bodies. Octopuses and squid have lots of flexible, writhing tentacles to grab food.

Worms live almost everywhere. **Roundworms** or nematodes are little more than digestive tubes. Some are smaller than the dot on this "i"—there could be 10,000 in a handful of soil.

Fanworms are relatives of earthworms. Their fantastic feathery arms collect tiny floating food bits in the water. This way of eating is called filter feeding. The worm's main body is in the tube buried in the sand.

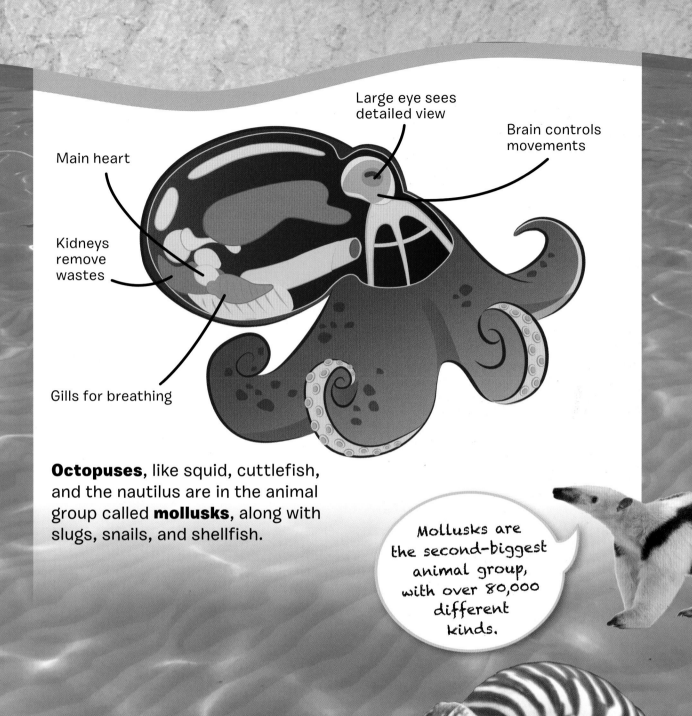

Large eye sees detailed view

Brain controls movements

Main heart

Kidneys remove wastes

Gills for breathing

Octopuses, like squid, cuttlefish, and the nautilus are in the animal group called **mollusks**, along with slugs, snails, and shellfish.

Mollusks are the second-biggest animal group, with over 80,000 different kinds.

Deep-sea **survivor**

Creatures almost exactly the same as the nautilus lived in the sea 400 million years ago, long before the dinosaurs. This mollusk catches fish with its grabbing tentacles—it has up to 90 of the long feelers!

Sliming around

Animals without a *skeleton* have many ways of moving around. One is by tightening muscles around blood or fluid in a body part, making it stiff and hard. In this way they can wriggle, squirm, and slither.

A **slug's** underside is called its foot. Its rows of muscles get shorter and longer, like waves in the sea, as the slug slides along on its own layer of slime. The slug on the left is going backwards.

The **squid** blasts along like a jet engine—backward! It gently sucks in water through a wide body opening, then squirts it out fast through a tube called a siphon.

Squirting this way ...

... sends the squid that way

The seashore **ragworm** is an animal rowboat. It has lines of flaps along its sides like tiny oars. They wave to and fro to paddle and row along, through water or even in sand and mud.

How it works

A **worm** is so strong that it can push its way through soil, making a tunnel as it burrows. It has a special technique for burrowing:

1) The rear part of the body gets wider to hold itself in the tunnel.
2) The front end becomes longer and thinner, forcing the worm forward.
3) The front widens to hold onto the soil, while the rear pulls up behind it.

If I had no skeleton of bones I'd flop down like a lump of Jell-O!

Slippery food

Apart from sponges, all animals have inner parts that digest or break down food. These usually include a stomach to hold the meal and begin digestion, and *intestines* to take in the nutrients.

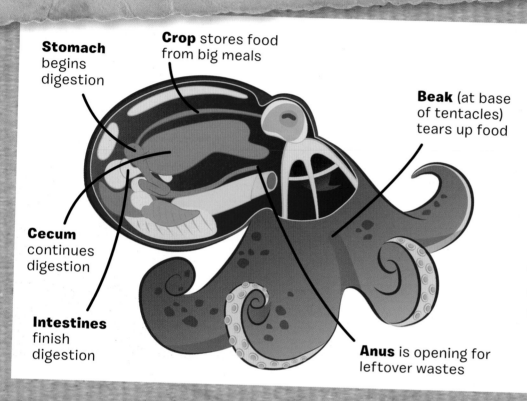

Stomach begins digestion

Crop stores food from big meals

Beak (at base of tentacles) tears up food

Cecum continues digestion

Intestines finish digestion

Anus is opening for leftover wastes

After grabbing a fish or crab with its tentacles, the **octopus** tears it apart with its parrot-like *beak*. It swallows the pieces into its many-part digestive tube. The leftover wastes come out of an opening on the side of its head!

Flatworms are leaf shaped and many are see-through. The stomach (which stores food) and intestine (which digests food) are the same as each other, with branches into all body parts.

I feed by licking up ants and termites with my very long tongue— two licks per second!

The **barnacle** stands on its head and kicks food into its mouth! The part fixed to a seashore rock is its head end. The feathers are really legs that sweep tiny bits of food into its stomach.

Chapter 3: Creepy-Crawlies
Hard on the outside

We have a skeleton inside us with muscles around it. Some creatures are the opposite—they have a hard outer skeleton with muscles inside it. They also have legs with *joints*. They are **arthropods**—the most common creatures on Earth.

Spiders and **scorpions** have eight legs—and *venom*. Scorpions have a venomous tail sting; spiders have venomous fangs. Other venomous animals include jellyfish, fish, and snakes.

Main groups of arthropods

- Bees, butterflies, beetles, and other **insects**
- Spiders, scorpions, mites, ticks—**arachnids**
- Horseshoe crabs—**merostomata**
- Crabs, lobsters, prawns, shrimps, barnacles, water fleas, woodlice—**crustaceans**
- Centipedes—**chilopods**
- Millipedes—**diplopods**

Orb-web spider

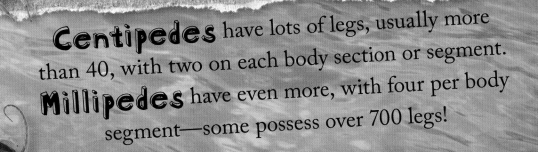

Centipedes have lots of legs, usually more than 40, with two on each body section or segment. **Millipedes** have even more, with four per body segment—some possess over 700 legs!

Many **insects** go through several stages in their lives. The dragonfly nymph, or larva, lives in water for a year or two. It then crawls out to shed its skin and become a winged adult—and dies within a few hours.

Common clubtail dragonfly emerging from larva

Lobsters are big, tough crustaceans. They have ten "legs"—eight for walking and swimming, and two shaped as *pincers* to grab food.

My favorite arthropods are ants and termites!

Legs on the move

Insects and other arthropods use their legs to move around in all kinds of ways. Each leg is like a hard tube, thinner and bendy at the joints, and with muscles inside.

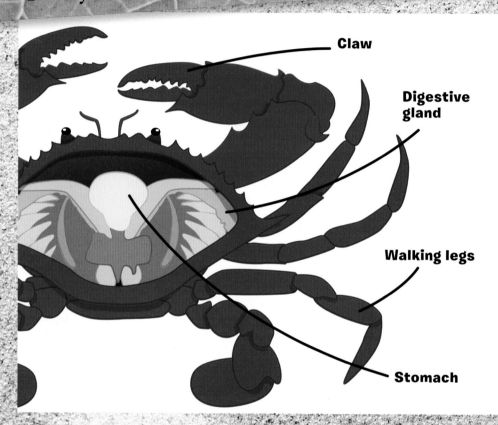

Claw

Digestive gland

Walking legs

Stomach

Each of a **crab's** legs has 10 joints and a sharp claw at the end. The crab is odd because its legs move from left to right, not forward and backward. So it runs sideways!

Lots of legs might seem difficult to control! They move forward and backward in waves along each side of the body so the **millipede** never trips over its own feet.

Lifted legs move forward

Lowered legs push backward

Most insects have wings as well as legs. One of the fastest fliers is the **dragonfly**. Its two pairs of big, strong wings flap up and down, and also twist and tilt to change direction and even let the insect hover.

My longest part is my nose—specially adapted to sniff out ants' nests!

Longest **legs**

The longest limbs of any arthropod belong to the giant spider crab. They stretch almost 6 ft. 6 in.!

Very sensible

Most insects and other arthropods have senses of sight, hearing, smell, taste, and touch. They also have body parts called feelers or antennae. These do not just feel: they can detect smells, tastes, and moving air too.

Insects' **eyes** like this fly's have many tiny, separate units. Each one sees a small part of the scene. The fly's brain adds them all together, like making a mosaic or jigsaw.

Seeing the **invisible**

Bees' eyes see what our eyes cannot. They detect ultraviolet rays which, on some flowers, show lines on the petals leading to sweet nectar.

A zinnia as seen by a human (above), and how it would look if seen by a bee (below).

Insects are so weird— but tasty too!

Not all animals' **ears** are on their head. The grasshopper's ears are on its knees. These thin flaps vibrate when they are hit by sound waves. Grasshoppers need their flaps to hear each other's chirps.

A cave cricket's **antennae** can be three times longer than its whole body! They wave around in the dark cave, touch the surroundings, and detect air movements. Eyes are not much use in darkness so some cave crickets are blind.

Eating machines

Small creatures like insects spend most of their time finding food, eating it, and avoiding danger. Different kinds bite, chew, munch, crunch, lick, and suck almost every food available, from solid wood to animal blood!

Spiders stab venom into their victims to kill them or to stop them from moving. The spider then oozes a liquid from its mouth that digests the meal by dissolving it, and laps up the resulting animal soup.

Bloodthirsty!

Many insects and other arthropods have sharp, stiff mouthparts which they use to suck blood, from which they get all the nourishment they need. Such insects include fleas, lice, bedbugs, mites, and ticks.

Scorpions grab food with their pincers, then tear it to bits with their powerful mouthparts. There are three cutting sections in their mouths and these work like scissors, moving from side to side to snip up the prey.

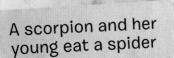

A scorpion and her young eat a spider

The long, tube-shaped mouth of a **butterfly** is called a proboscis. Usually it's coiled in a spiral under the butterfly's head. It straightens out like a drinking straw to poke into flowers and suck the sugary nectar.

Crabs have a complicated way of eating and digesting their food. A crab's mouth has three sets of "jaws" and its stomach contains hard lumps and bumps which are used to grind food into a mush.

First set of **mouthparts** holds food

Second set of mouthparts tears food

Third set of mouthparts pushes food into stomach

Hard plates inside **stomach** mash food

Intestines' powerful **juices** digest food

Digestive gland takes food into body

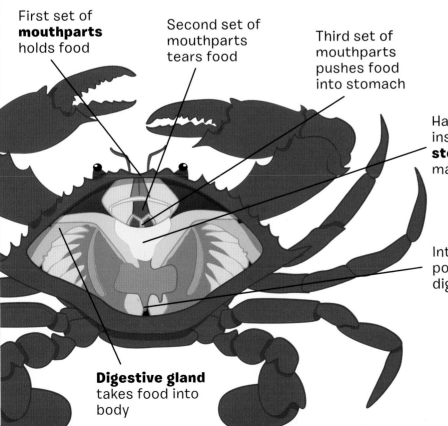

I'm like a crab—my stomach also has hard lumps inside to grind up my food. You won't catch me walking sideways though!

29

Watery world

The see-through skin of this **glass catfish** allows us to see its inner parts. We can clearly see its long backbone with spines radiating up and down. Swimming muscles surround the bone.

Fish "breathe" through **gills**. Water comes in through the mouth and flows over the gills, and the oxygen in it passes to the blood flowing through the gills. The water then flows out through the gill slits on the neck.

Gills visible inside a grouper's mouth

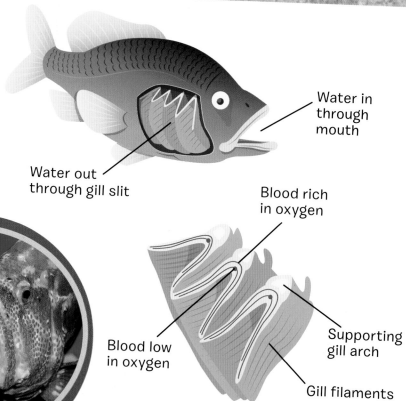

Water in through mouth

Water out through gill slit

Blood rich in oxygen

Blood low in oxygen

Supporting gill arch

Gill filaments

Most fish have a backbone and inner skeleton including jaws for eating and gills for breathing under water. They have fins to aid movement, and skin covered with *scales* for protection. But there are exceptions—eels and catfish have no scales, and lungfish can breathe out of water.

Big fish, little fish

The **whale shark** is huge, similar to the size of a bus, at 39 ft. 4 in. long and 22 tons in weight. In contrast, a pygmy goby is a real tiddler, at less than ½ in. long and barely weighing anything.

Some fish can exist out of water for short lengths of time. The **mudskipper** has large gill chambers that hold enough water to let it breathe in air for a while. It also has strong front fins which it uses like arms to move over mud and rocks.

I can breathe in water by poking my nose above the surface like a snorkel!

Fins 'n' tails

Fish use fins like we use our legs. The number of fins a fish has is usually between one and 10, but sometimes more.

Old four-legs

The **coelacanth** has *pectoral* (chest) and *pelvic* (underneath at front of fish) fins with flesh and muscle at the base. They are similar to the legs of the very early land animals that appeared on Earth more than 300 million years ago.

Rays do not so much swim as "fly" through the water. The ray's pectoral (side) fins are like big, fleshy "wings" that wave up and down, while its tail is long and thin and trails along behind.

The **manta** is the biggest ray, 19 ft. 8 in. long and the same across.

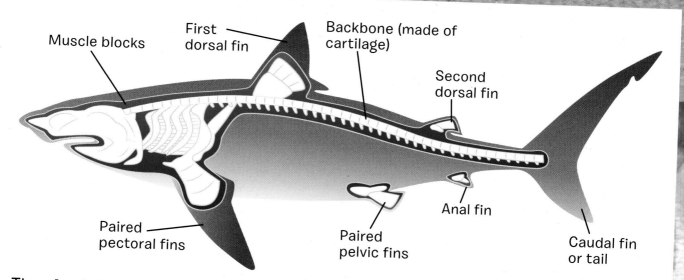

Muscle blocks

First dorsal fin

Backbone (made of cartilage)

Second dorsal fin

Anal fin

Caudal fin or tail

Paired pelvic fins

Paired pectoral fins

The **shark** has all of the main fins that other fish have, but the shark's fins have muscles inside and are not as bendy as the fins of other fish. Large muscles that run along each side of a shark's body are used to move the tail fin.

Flying fish leap from the water to escape predators. They do not really fly, like birds, but they do glide many feet in the air, using their wide, stretched-out side fins.

I have a tail, but I use it to keep warm, not to swim!

Fishy senses

The fish's world is very different to our living conditions on land. The sea gets darker with depth, sounds go faster, currents push animals around, and scents and tastes seem very similar to each other. Plus there are tiny pulses of electricity all around in the water!

A **shark's** head has hundreds of tiny pores called ampullae. These ampullae sense small bursts of electricity that are created naturally by the muscles of other animals. The electricity sparks travel really well through water and help the shark to hunt for prey.

Sharks' **senses** for attack

3,281 ft. or more—**smell**
164 ft.—**sight**
65 ft.—**water ripples and currents**
16 ft.—**electrical pulses**
0 ft.—**taste!**

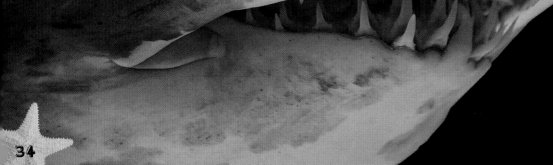

Most fish have a sensitive stripe along each side of the body, called the lateral line. This line detects ripples and currents of moving water, alerting the fish to possible danger—the ripples could be caused by other creatures moving nearby.

Gray snapper

Deeper than 1,640 ft. in the ocean, there is no sunlight, just complete darkness. Some fish make their own light using body parts called photophores. These lights shine to see prey or predators, or flash on and off to attract a mate for breeding.

Lanternfish have huge eyes and small photophores (see left) along their sides.

Sometimes I see light-making animals. They are glowworms, and are actually varieties of beetle.

Fishy food

From the smallest pond to the deepest ocean, watery habitats are full of things to eat. With more than 30,000 kinds of fish, there is one specialized to eat almost every type of food.

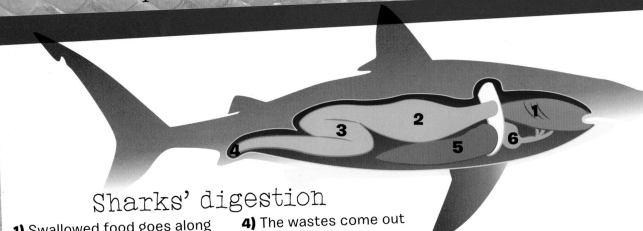

Sharks' digestion

1) Swallowed food goes along the **gullet** into the stomach.

2) The **stomach** digests the food.

3) The **intestines** take the resulting nutrients and send them to the liver.

4) The wastes come out of the **vent**.

5) The **liver** stores and alters the nutrients and sends them into the blood.

6) The **heart** pumps blood around the body.

Predatory fish, such as **moray eels**, usually have sharp teeth to kill and cut pieces off their victims. They can strike or bite with great speed.

The **X-ray tetra** has see-through skin and scales. Its stomach, intestines, heart, and other organs are packed into the area behind the head. The organs of most fish are organized like this inside.

Whale fall

A **whale fall** is a dead whale that sinks to the seabed. It is a giant feast for worms, crabs, shellfish, and many fish, including the huge 20 ft.-long sleeper shark, which loves dead meat.

The mosquito fish is useful. It eats the water-living young, or larvae, of pesky biting mosquitoes.

Parrotfish

scrape coral reef rocks with their hard, tough, beak-like mouths to eat tiny plants and animals. Bits of rock may also come away. These are then swallowed. The particles pass through the fish and are expelled as dazzling grains of coral sand!

Chapter 5: Best of Both Worlds
Air and water

Amphibian animals begin life in water. Then many move out of the water to live on land—and change their body parts as they go. They include frogs and toads, newts and salamanders, and the strange caecilians, which look like worms.

Most amphibians like the watery conditions of ponds, damp ditches, and even soggy undergrowth. However, the **water-holding frog** lives in the desert—but it stays underground and only comes out after rain.

Baby amphibians are called tadpoles. They live in water—even a little puddle of rain trapped in a leaf or a flower is big enough for them to exist in.

Baby tadpoles have frilly gills to breathe in water. But in a few weeks these shrivel and the lungs in the body start working. This also means the grown-up can make noises—"croak," "rivet," "peep"!

Caecilians are amphibians but they look like worms or snakes. Caecilians do not need legs: they burrow in soil like earthworms. They are fierce predators and gobble up any small creatures they find.

I rarely see frogs in my grassland home, but around the world there are almost 5,000 different kinds!

Hop off!

Amphibians have lots of ways of getting around. Frogs hop, toads walk, salamanders waddle, and newts wriggle—and they can all swim.

Frogs, like fish, reptiles, birds, and mammals, have an inner skeleton. Muscles attached to the bones pull on them to make them move. A frog's rear leg bones are long and the muscles are very powerful, so the frog can make great leaps.

When **leaping**, a frog's front legs are just as important as its back ones. They stretch forward and bend upon touchdown to soften the landing. If they didn't, the frog would crash on its chin.

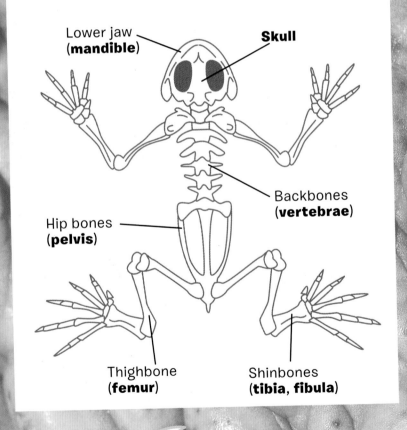

Lower jaw (**mandible**)

Skull

Backbones (**vertebrae**)

Hip bones (**pelvis**)

Thighbone (**femur**)

Shinbones (**tibia, fibula**)

A froggy friend told me the world record for a frog leap is well over 16 ft. 4 in.!

Newts swim by waving their long, broad tails from side to side, like fish, but their feet are small and much better suited to walking on land.

Flying feet

The frog's **webbed feet** are designed for swimming—or gliding. The flying tree frog opens them like parachutes as it swoops down from a branch, usually to flee predators.

Gulp it down

All adult amphibians are meat-eaters. But they do not bite off big lumps of fleshy meat. Their usual food consists of creatures like flies, worms, and slugs, all swallowed alive!

A **frog** has the usual digestive parts of a gullet, stomach, and intestines. But these have to work extra-hard. The frog cannot chew its meal to make it softer— so it swallows every victim whole.

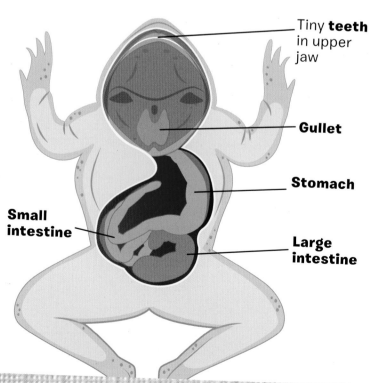

Tiny **teeth** in upper jaw

Gullet

Stomach

Small intestine

Large intestine

Big frogs and toads like **bullfrogs** are strong, with a wide mouth and powerful bite. They can eat small lizards, birds, and even mice!

Young **tadpoles** usually eat plants before they become meat-eating frogs. Their intestines show through the thin skin of the belly as a long, coiled tube.

Sticky-tipped tongue

Some frogs have a tongue as long as their body! They flick it out in a flash to catch a fly on its sticky tip, and then pull the tongue back in to swallow the food.

My tongue is much longer than a frog's—over 20 in.!

All change!

Amphibians go through great changes as they grow up. This change of shape is called **metamorphosis** and happens inside the body as well as on the outside.

Frog life cycle

1) The adult female frog lays jelly-covered **eggs**, called frog spawn.

2) The eggs hatch into **tadpoles** with frilly gills and a long tail.

3) The gills and tail shrink and the lungs and legs develop.

4) The tadpole is now a **froglet**.

5) The froglet grows larger and becomes an adult.

Eggs

Embryos

Adult frog

Tadpoles with legs

Froglet

The **axolotl** is a salamander that "never grows up." It develops legs and small lungs but keeps its tadpole-stage feathery gills and long tail.

The male **midwife toad** does not leave the eggs on their own. He guards them by carrying them around on his body, and dips them into puddles or ponds to keep them wet.

Piggyback **babies**

The female **Suriname toad** lays *eggs* that the male puts onto her back. Once the eggs are on the female's back, a flap of skin grows over each one and a tadpole develops in a pocket underneath. After a few weeks, it comes out looking just like a mini-toad!

Some frogs lay over 3,000 eggs! Luckily anteaters have only one baby at a time.

Chapter 6: Super-Scaly
Outer armor

The most obvious feature of a **reptile** is its outer covering. This may be lots of overlapping scales, like a lizard or a snake, or it could be a strong domed shell, like a turtle or tortoise. It might even consist of thick scales and lumps of bone, like a crocodile or alligator.

Lizards live in almost every habitat—even the hottest deserts. To avoid getting burned feet, these desert dwellers raise two legs off the hot sand at a time, then put those two down and lift up the other two.

A bearded agama lizard from Australia

There are over 10,000 kinds of reptiles—and 6,000 are lizards.

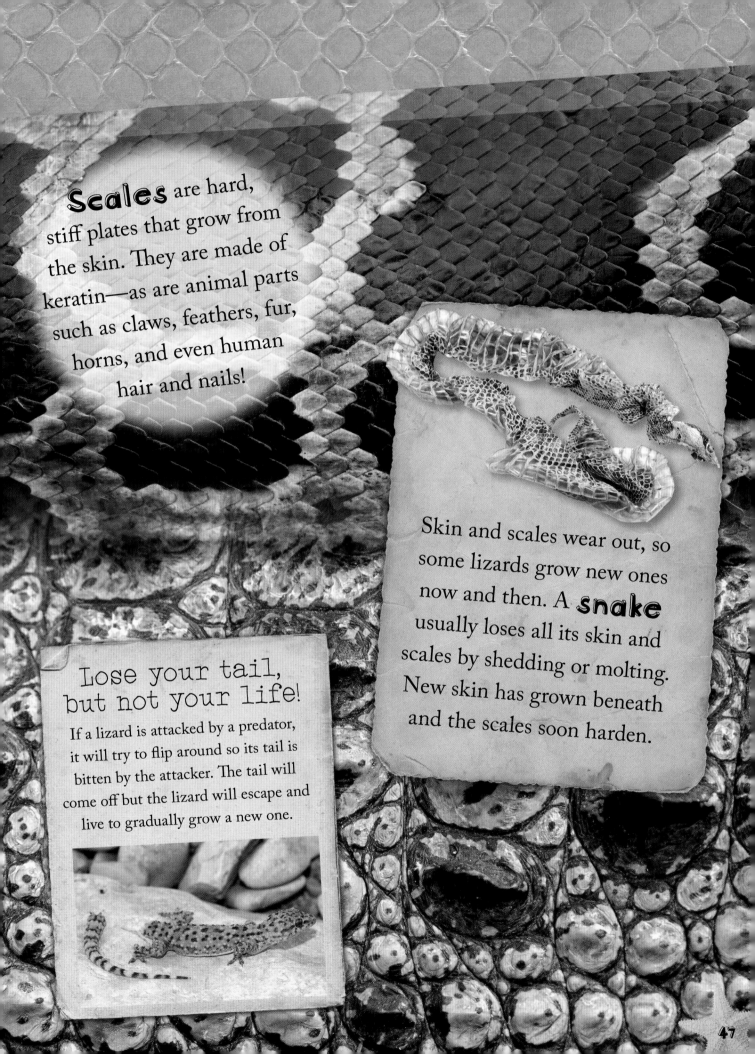

Scales are hard, stiff plates that grow from the skin. They are made of keratin—as are animal parts such as claws, feathers, fur, horns, and even human hair and nails!

Skin and scales wear out, so some lizards grow new ones now and then. A **snake** usually loses all its skin and scales by shedding or molting. New skin has grown beneath and the scales soon harden.

Lose your tail, but not your life!

If a lizard is attacked by a predator, it will try to flip around so its tail is bitten by the attacker. The tail will come off but the lizard will escape and live to gradually grow a new one.

Walking or sliding

Reptiles get around in many different ways. They have an inner skeleton of bones pulled by muscles, and most have legs to walk or run. Snakes have no legs but they can slither, burrow, climb, and swim, and a few can even "fly"!

The biggest **crocodiles** grow to over 19 ft. 8 in. long and weigh more than one ton. Even so, they can run very fast using their powerful leg muscles, swinging their bodies from side to side.

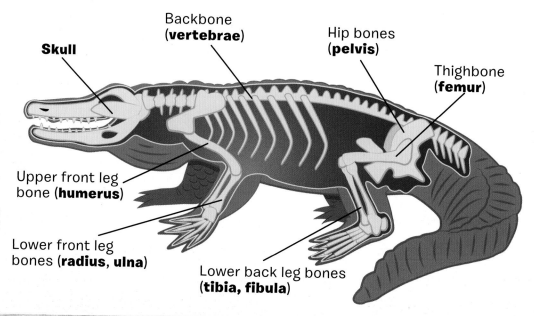

Skull

Backbone (**vertebrae**)

Hip bones (**pelvis**)

Thighbone (**femur**)

Upper front leg bone (**humerus**)

Lower front leg bones (**radius**, **ulna**)

Lower back leg bones (**tibia**, **fibula**)

Turtles and **tortoises** have very strange skeletons. Their backbones and rib bones are wide and curved on the insides of their shells. On the outside of each shell are plates called scutes. The whole shell is very strong—but it makes these reptiles slow.

Going **sideways?**

Some snakes move by moving their bodies from side to side, called **sidewinding**. They lift the front of the body, place it down at an angle, slide part-forward and part-sideways, lift the front end again, and so on. This method allows the snake to grip the ground well in soft sand.

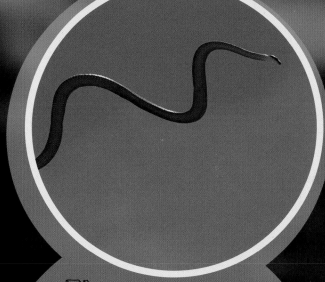

Flying snakes

do not truly fly but they can glide a very long way down from the treetops. The snake makes its rib bones tilt out, so its tube-shaped body widens into a flatter ribbon shape.

Forget scales: I'm quite happy with my long fur–cool in summer, warm in winter. The perfect coat!

Touchy, feely, tasty

Reptiles have the usual sensing parts—eyes, ears, nose, tongue, and skin. Some also have heat detectors that can "see" in the dark.

A **pit viper** has hole-like pits between its eyes and nose. These sense heat coming from warm-blooded animals like birds and mammals. This means the viper can find its next meal even in total darkness.

Heat-sensing pit

Unlike most animals, the **chameleon's** eyes work separately. They point up, down, forward, and backward. So this lizard can see in front and behind at the same time!

A chameleon's eyes can look different ways.

A snake smelling the air by tongue

Snakes and lizards "smell" with their **tongues**. The tongue flicks out and collects tiny smell particles floating in the air, then flicks back in and places these particles on a sensitive part of the roof of the mouth.

Komodo dragons are the biggest lizards, 9 ft. 10 in. long. They love the stench of death—they can smell rotting meat three miles away!

The Komodo dragon is short compared to the longest snake, the 22-ft.-long reticulated python.

Spear 'n' snap

Unlike mammals and birds, reptiles are cold-blooded. Since they do not have to use food to make body heat, they eat less often. A big meal can keep a crocodile going for three months!

Crocodiles swallow big chunks of meat into their huge stomachs. They swallow stones, too, called **gastrolith stones**. The stones help weigh the animal down so it floats low in the water and can stay hidden. They also help to grind and mash the meat in the stomach—even the bones.

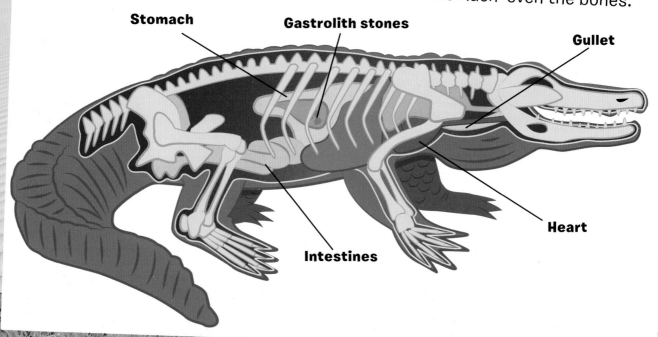

Stomach

Gastrolith stones

Gullet

Heart

Intestines

A snapping turtle eating a raccoon

Turtles do not have teeth—but they do have very sharp jaw edges. Like a bird's strong beak, these cut and slice food. The snapping turtle can easily bite a fish in half!

About 600 kinds of snakes have **Venom**, which they stab into their prey with their long teeth, called fangs. Venomous snakes include cobras, adders, mambas, sea snakes, and vipers like the rattlesnake. The venom is made by venom glands next to the snake's jawbones.

The **thorny devil** is a fierce-looking lizard with scales like sharp prickles and thorns for protection. But it is really quite peaceful and eats ants, termites, and small bugs.

The thorny devil lives in Australia, so it can't steal my ants!

Eggs galore

Most baby reptiles hatch from **eggs**. Unlike a bird's hard eggshell, a reptile's eggshell is soft and bendy, like leather. Most mother reptiles lay their eggs and leave them. The babies are left to develop in the eggs and when they hatch out, they are on their own!

The mother **sea turtle** crawls onto the beach to dig a hole where she lays her eggs—sometimes 100 eggs or more. Then she covers them with sand and returns to the sea.

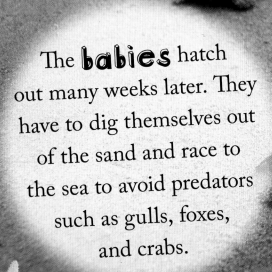

The **babies** hatch out many weeks later. They have to dig themselves out of the sand and race to the sea to avoid predators such as gulls, foxes, and crabs.

Inside a **reptile's egg** is the developing baby, called an *embryo*. It is protected by coverings or membranes and has a store of food in the yolk sac.

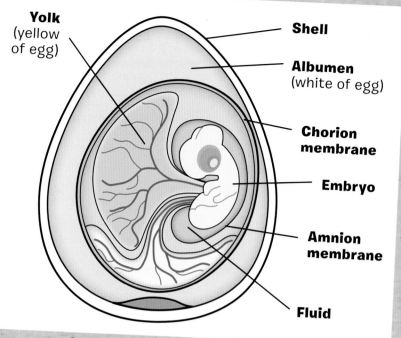

Yolk (yellow of egg)

Shell

Albumen (white of egg)

Chorion membrane

Embryo

Amnion membrane

Fluid

Reptiles' eggshells have to be tough to protect the babies inside. So every baby has a sharp, tooth-like part which is called an egg tooth. The baby uses it to break a hole in the egg so that it can come out, then the egg tooth falls off.

Pueblan milk snake hatching from its egg, Mexico

There are only 24 kinds of crocs, alligators, and caimans, but they are the biggest reptiles.

The **best** mother

Only a few reptiles care for their babies. A female crocodile or alligator makes a nest for the eggs, helps the babies to hatch, carries them to water, and guards them for months. With such a fierce mother, few predators dare to attack!

Chapter 7: In the Air
Rulers of the skies

Only three kinds of animal are truly masters of flight—insects, bats, and birds. The birds are the biggest and best fliers, with every part of the body designed to save weight and maximize their skills in the air.

A bird's **bones** are hollow, which makes the bird light. The bird's lungs breathe in air which flows into hollow air sacs, again keeping the bird as light as possible.

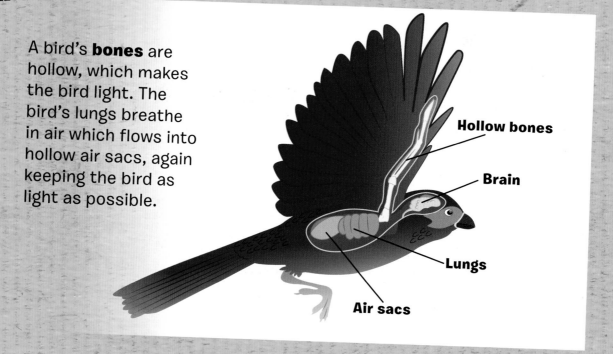

Hollow bones

Brain

Lungs

Air sacs

A swan's webbed feet

As well as flying, some birds are expert **swimmers**. The swan has flaps of skin called webs between its toes. Webbed feet are much better than separate toes for pushing against the water, so they help the swan to paddle faster.

The bird that flies most is the **swift**. It may stay in the air for an entire year, feeding on small flying insects and swooping down to sip water from ponds. It can even lightly doze on the wing!

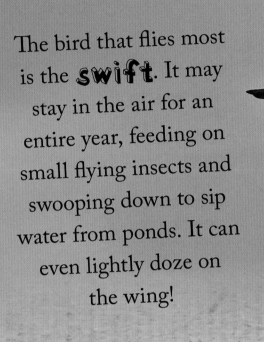

Birds have **scales** like reptiles—but only on their legs, for protection. They have claws, too, which are long and strong in birds of prey like the hawk.

There are about 10,000 kinds of birds—almost twice as many as us mammals!

Flying high

If we relate a bird's skeleton to a human skeleton, a bird's wings are its arms, and the bones inside are designed for flight. Feathers grow from the skin and are super-light yet perfectly formed to push the air well. A large bird has 20,000 of them!

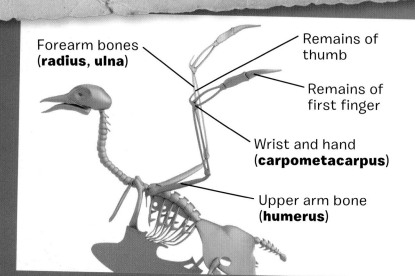

Forearm bones (**radius, ulna**)

Remains of thumb

Remains of first finger

Wrist and hand (**carpometacarpus**)

Upper arm bone (**humerus**)

The **arm bones** of a bird are specially designed for flight. There are no proper finger or hand bones, just one tiny thumb and what is left of the first finger.

Two sets of muscles, both in the chest, power a bird's flight. The wing feathers also move.

Upstroke
The feathers tilt to allow air through, and smaller chest muscles that run up over the bird's shoulders contract to lift the wings.

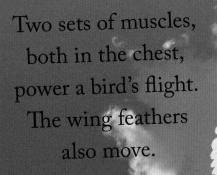

Downstroke
The feathers form an airtight surface as the main chest muscles pull the wings down and back, pushing the bird up and forward.

Large wingtip feathers, called **primaries**, spread out and tilt for greater control in the air.

Main wing feathers, called **secondaries**, produce the lifting force to keep the bird up in the air.

Flying underwater

Penguins cannot fly in air—but they can in water. They use an up-and-down flapping motion to swim—and they can swim as fast as you can run!

The fastest creature in the world is the peregrine falcon, which power-dives at 197 ft. each second!

Eagle-eyed

Birds have big *brains*, with especially large parts for sight, movement, and balance. Most birds are clever and learn fast—a parrot can learn to do as many tricks as a pet dog!

Inside an **eagle's eye** is a lens that bends light rays to give a sharp, clear view. This falls on the retina, which changes light rays to nerve signals for the brain.

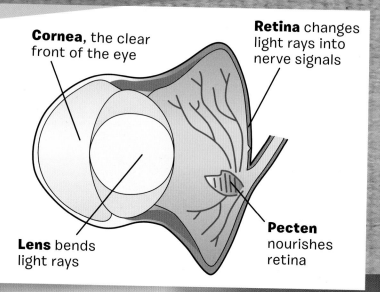

Cornea, the clear front of the eye

Retina changes light rays into nerve signals

Lens bends light rays

Pecten nourishes retina

To see in near-darkness, the owl's huge eyes fill more than half its head. They cannot move in their bowl-like sockets so the owl must turn its head instead. It can twist its neck right around to look behind!

A great horned owl

vultures who are able to detect dead meat from miles away. The nostrils on a bird are usually at the beak's base. But the **kiwi's** nostrils are at the tip of its beak, so it can sniff out small soil creatures for food.

A kiwi sniffing for food

Black woodpecker using its long tongue

The **woodpecker** has a very long tongue. Its bristly end pokes under bark and into woody holes to pull out tasty bugs.

I like the woodpecker—any animal with a long tongue is my friend!

61

Peck, peck

Teeth are heavy. Instead, a bird has a lightweight **beak**, sometimes called a bill, made of a strong, horny material. Birds' beaks come in a huge range of shapes and sizes, from as short as a rice grain to as long as your arm!

The shape or design of a bird's beak gives an idea of what it eats. The **parrot** has a strong beak with a sharp tip—perfect for cracking nuts and slicing open the tough fruits that it likes to eat.

A flamingo's beak works best upside down

Pelicans have the biggest beaks. They are over 17 in. long. The chin of loose skin on the bottom of its beak fills like a balloon with water and fishy food. Then the pelican squeezes out the water and swallows down the big, yummy meal.

A bird has **three stomach-like parts**. The first is the large storage bag, called the crop. Next is the actual stomach, which contains powerful digestive juices. Then comes the gizzard, where strong muscles mash the food into a soup-like liquid.

Stomach
(proventriculus)

Gizzard
(ventriculus)

Gullet

Crop

Intestine

Keep it crossed

The **crossbill** has a cross-tipped beak. It uses the unusual shape to push apart the scaly flaps on pine and fir cones to get at the delicious seeds inside. These are one of its favorite snacks.

The beak of the swordbill hummingbird is 4 in.—longer than its head and body!

Nest eggs

All birds lay **eggs** and nearly all birds look after their babies, called chicks, when they hatch. Being a parent bird is tiring. The chicks seem to be permanently open-mouthed and squawking for food!

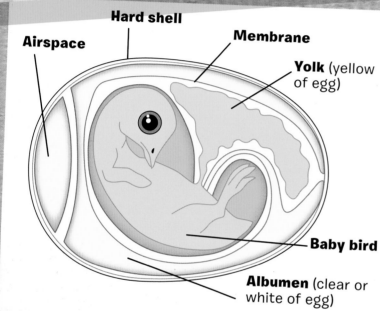

Airspace

Hard shell

Membrane

Yolk (yellow of egg)

Baby bird

Albumen (clear or white of egg)

A bird's **egg** has a hard shell. It protects the fertilized egg, which is called the embryo. The yellow part of the egg is a food store, called the yolk. The clear matter within the eggshell is albumen, which both protects and feeds the baby.

At breeding time, many male birds call and sing, shake and show off their feathers, and even jump or dance about. They do this to attract females. The most extravagant displays are by male **birds of paradise**.

Garden birds like robins make bowl-shaped nests of twigs, stems, leaves, and moss. One parent sits on the eggs to protect them and keep them warm, known as **incubation**, while the other goes off to feed.

Parent **eagles** tear and rip the animals they catch, and feed the pieces to their chicks. Some birds eat food, part-digest it, and then bring it up again for their babies—yeugh!

Swan chicks, known as **cygnets**, are able to swim just hours after they hatch. But they also like to ride on the mother's back, where they are safer.

Eggs-ellent
record-breakers

Biggest egg	Ostrich, 7 in. long
Smallest egg	Vervain hummingbird, ⅜ in. long
Most eggs	Bobwhite quail, 28
Fewest eggs	Albatross, 1 (every two years)

I like nests too—the termite nests I break open with my big claws!

Chapter 8: Warm and Furry
Creatures like us

Most animals we see around are mammals. They are warm-blooded, they have live babies, they feed their babies on mother's milk, and they have fur or hair.

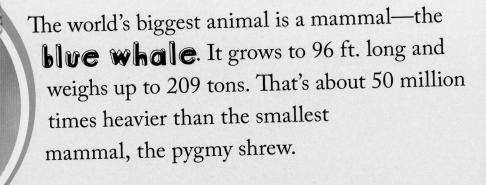

A pygmy shrew weighs 2-6 grams

The world's biggest animal is a mammal—the **blue whale**. It grows to 96 ft. long and weighs up to 209 tons. That's about 50 million times heavier than the smallest mammal, the pygmy shrew.

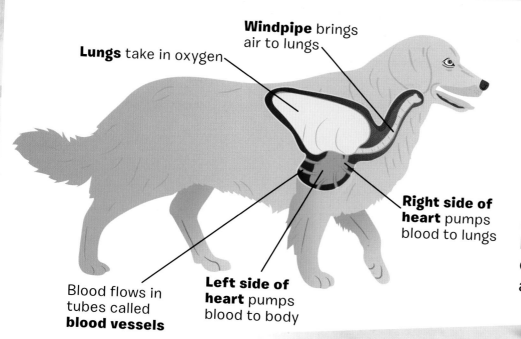

Lungs take in oxygen

Windpipe brings air to lungs

Right side of heart pumps blood to lungs

Blood flows in tubes called **blood vessels**

Left side of heart pumps blood to body

Mammals have a big **heart** in proportion to their body size. The heart pumps blood to the lungs to take in oxygen, then pushes the blood around the body to deliver the oxygen to its organs and cells.

Being **warm-blooded** means that mammals can stay active in the coldest places, even near the North Pole. But it also means they have to eat lots of food in order to generate enough body warmth.

I have a low temperature for a mammal, 91.4°F. More usual is 96.8–104°F.

Mammal **eggs?**

Only a few mammals lay eggs—the **platypus**, and **echidnas** or spiny anteaters. When the babies hatch, the mother feeds them with her milk, like other mammals. An egg-laying mammal is called a **monotreme**.

Short-beaked echidna

Furry, hairy

Even "hairless" mammals like elephants, rhinos, whales, and dolphins have a few bristly hairs here and there—mainly there!

Fur, hairs, bristles, whiskers—even the porcupine's sharp quills—all develop in the same way. Each strand grows from a pouch-like pocket in the skin called a follicle. Only the base or root of the strand is alive. The shaft of the hair or fur is dead. That's why it doesn't hurt when your hair is cut!

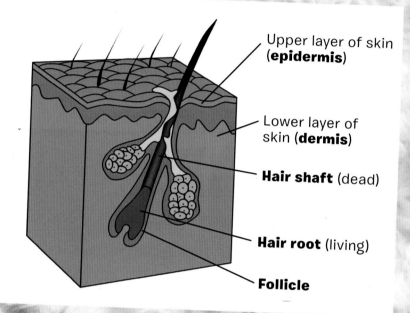

Upper layer of skin (**epidermis**)

Lower layer of skin (**dermis**)

Hair shaft (dead)

Hair root (living)

Follicle

A fur coat is very important. It keeps the body warm and dry, protecting it from all weathers. No wonder mammals like the **otter** spend so long *grooming* their fur to get rid of tangles, dirt, and pests.

The **naked mole rat** lives underground and has almost no fur. But it does have extra-long snout hairs called whiskers, which help the mole rat to find its way through the dark tunnels it lives in.

The **pangolin** or scaly anteater looks like a scaly reptile but its "scales" are like big, flat hairs, made of the same material, keratin, with some thin hairs in between.

Like many mammals, I molt or shed my hairs each year and grow a new fur coat.

Super-furry
The longest animal hairs are more than 3 ft. 3 in. and belong to **musk oxen**, who live in the ice and snow of the Arctic.

Bite to eat

With more than 5,000 kinds of mammals, there is one for almost every type of food. The fiercest feeders are meat-eaters, also called carnivores, like cats, wolves, foxes, stoats, and sea lions.

The long, fang-like **teeth** of a meat-eater, like this tiger, are called canines. They are used to rip and tear prey. The small teeth in front are incisors and these are great for nibbling and gnawing. The big, flat-topped rear teeth, or molars, can slice flesh and shear bones.

The **dog** has all the standard digestive parts of a mammal. Its stomach can hold lots of food, since wild dogs had to feast when they could, and might go for days without meals.

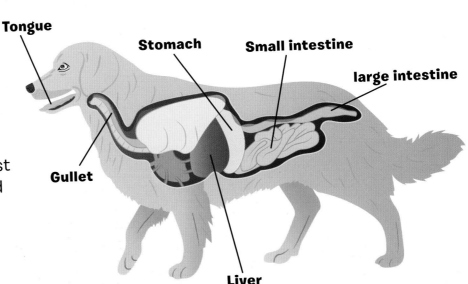

Tongue
Stomach
Small intestine
large intestine
Gullet
Liver

Seals' teeth are specially designed to hold slippery, squirming fish and squid. Their sharp points jab in and grip firmly, even through tough fish scales.

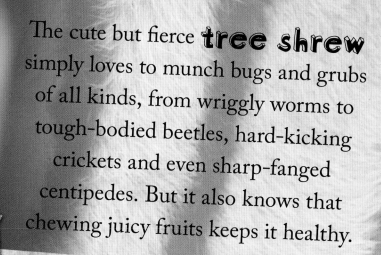

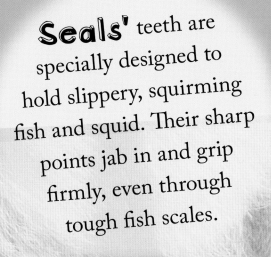

The cute but fierce **tree shrew** simply loves to munch bugs and grubs of all kinds, from wriggly worms to tough-bodied beetles, hard-kicking crickets and even sharp-fanged centipedes. But it also knows that chewing juicy fruits keeps it healthy.

I'm a big eater too—30,000 ants and termites each day.

Hungry hyena

The **hyena** has a huge appetite and a big stomach to match. It can gobble up 110 lb. in one meal—that's the same as 120 chicken legs!

Chomp 'n' chew

Plants contain fewer nutrients than meat. So mammal plant-eaters, called **herbivores**, eat much more than carnivores, and spend longer chewing and digesting food.

The **horse** is a herbivore. It has sharp front incisors, excellent for cutting off grass. Its rear teeth, or molars, are big and wide, and just perfect for hours of chewing. Horses do not have the fang-like canines that meat-eaters have.

A **rhino's** long lips help it to eat. The lips extend to grab plant food and pull it into the mouth for biting. These sorts of lips are called grasping, or prehensile, lips.

A **giraffe** can reach leaves up to 19 ft. 8 in. off the ground. It has long front legs, a long neck, and a tongue that is 1 ft. 6 in. long, which curls around food and pulls it into the animal's mouth.

Big **guts**

Manatees and **dugongs** are sirenians or "sea cows." Like cows on land, they eat grass—but sea grass and similar ocean plants. Manatees *graze* just like land cows, but to get enough goodness from the tough underwater food, their stomach and intestines are 98 ft. long!

An elephant eats 330 lb. of food daily, four times my weight!

Dugong accompanied by pilot jackfish

Super skills

Mammals have some of the best senses in the animal world. Each species has specialized senses for its habitat and lifestyle. For example, in thick forest, sight is limited, so smell and hearing are often more useful, alerting animals to danger—or dinner!

Hearing is a useful sense, especially on dark nights. In the Sahara Desert, the **fennec fox** sits still and listens out for very small creatures like lizards and insects. It turns its huge ears to track the tiny sound.

A **mammal's eye** is mainly a ball full of thick jelly. To see, light rays go through the hole, or pupil, in the iris, are then bent or focused by the lens, pass through the jelly, and get detected by the retina at the rear.

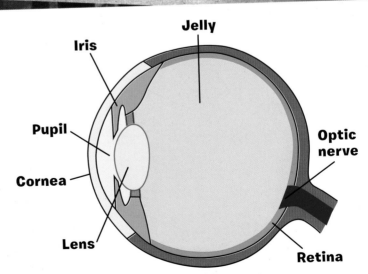

Jelly

Iris

Pupil

Cornea

Lens

Optic nerve

Retina

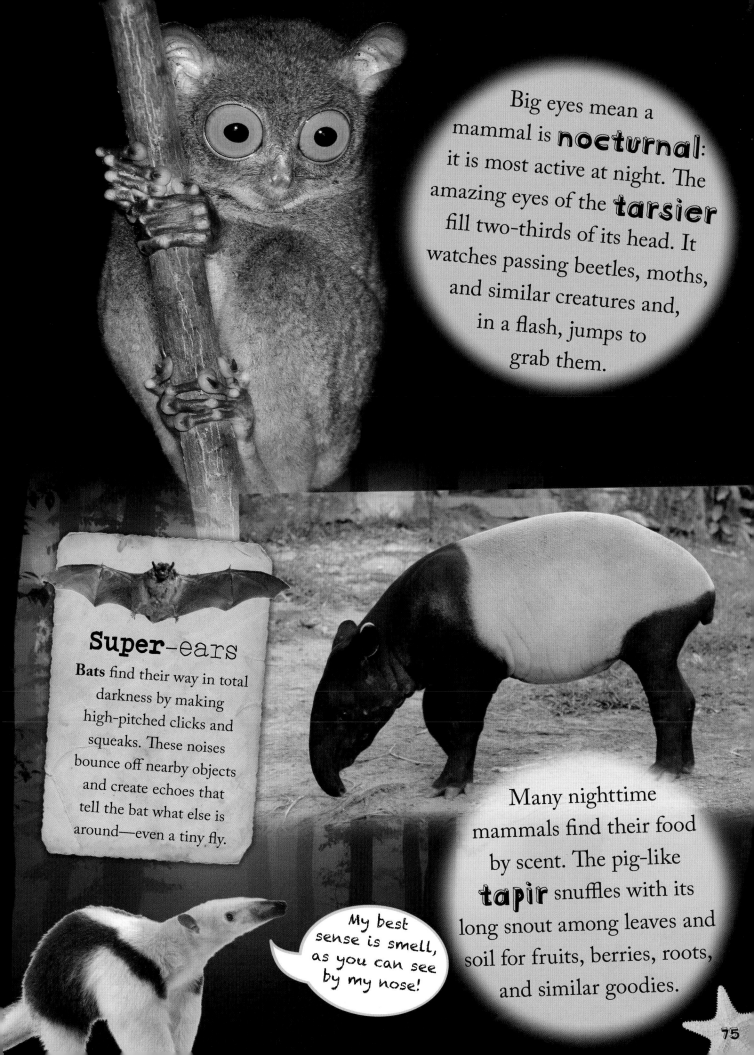

Big eyes mean a mammal is **nocturnal**: it is most active at night. The amazing eyes of the **tarsier** fill two-thirds of its head. It watches passing beetles, moths, and similar creatures and, in a flash, jumps to grab them.

Super-ears

Bats find their way in total darkness by making high-pitched clicks and squeaks. These noises bounce off nearby objects and create echoes that tell the bat what else is around—even a tiny fly.

My best sense is smell, as you can see by my nose!

Many nighttime mammals find their food by scent. The pig-like **tapir** snuffles with its long snout among leaves and soil for fruits, berries, roots, and similar goodies.

Arms and legs

All mammals have a skeleton made of bones that are attached to a web of muscles. Movement happens when the muscles pull the bones in a certain direction. Their ways of moving are endlessly varied: crawl, walk, run, dig, burrow, leap, glide, fly, dive, and swim.

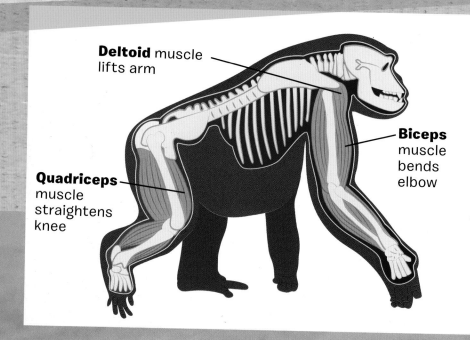

Deltoid muscle lifts arm

Quadriceps muscle straightens knee

Biceps muscle bends elbow

The **gorilla** has more muscle for its size than almost any other mammal. Long muscles in the arms and legs pull the bones. These move at joints: the shoulder, elbow, wrist, and fingers, and the hip, knee, ankle, and toes.

The **cheetah** is the world's fastest runner, with its slim yet muscular build, long legs, and long backbone too. The backbone arches up and down so the legs can reach even further with every bound.

I'm not speedy but I can easily walk 15 miles each day.

Some South American monkeys have five grasping limbs—two arms, two legs, and a tail. The **spider monkey** hangs by its tail alone, leaving its hands and feet free in order to feed.

Rapid **runners**

Cheetah 68 mph
Pronghorn 55 mph
Lion 49 mph
Hare 46 mph
Kangaroo 43 mph
Human 27 mph

No other animal moves like the **gibbon**. Its arms are longer than its legs and its hands are hook-shaped. The gibbon swings effortlessly through the forest's branches, much faster than any animal could run between the trees.

Flying without much flapping

The mammal called the flying lemur, or colugo, is not a lemur and cannot fly. But it is the best mammal glider, capable of swooping farther than 328 ft. from a tall tree. However, the only mammals that truly fly are bats.

The **bat's wing** is held out mostly by its very long finger bones, and is flapped up and down by big, strong chest muscles. Its short thumb has a claw for hanging at rest.

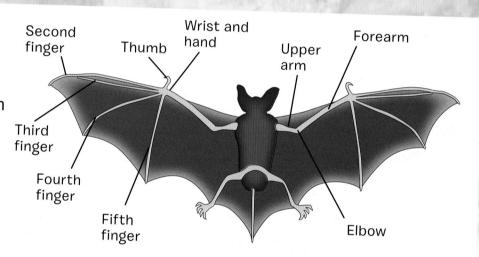

Second finger
Thumb
Wrist and hand
Upper arm
Forearm
Third finger
Fourth finger
Fifth finger
Elbow

Gambian epauletted fruit bat

Small bats hunt while they're in the air for flying insects like moths and beetles. Larger types of bat swoop down to grab frogs, lizards, mice, and even fish. The biggest bats are the **fruit bats** or flying foxes, which have dog-like faces. They feast on fruits, leaves, and flowers.

The **colugo** is a living parachute! It has thin flaps of skin stretching between its head, arms, legs, and tail. It usually leaps from a tree and glides away to avoid danger or to cross a clearing.

Fast fliers

Free-tailed bat 59 mph
Vampire bat 25 mph
Fruit bat 22 mph
Brown bat 16 mph
Colugo 12½ mph
Human 81 mph
(but only in a hang glider!)

The **sugar glider** is a marsupial or pouched mammal, and is a species related to kangaroos and koalas. Its furry flaps stretch along the sides of its body from hand to foot. It is called a "sugar" glider because it loves sweet nectar, flowers, and fruits.

The biggest fruit bats have wings almost 6 ft. 6 in. across, the same as my entire length from nose to tail!

Super-swimmers

Almost every mammal can **swim**, even if it's just to avoid drowning! But some mammals are experts in the water. The otter and the platypus have webbed feet for walking and for swimming. Other mammals have arms and legs shaped like flippers, perfect for moving in the water.

The **platypus** sticks its nose in riverbed mud and roots around with its beak-shaped snout for worms and similar food. Its long toes have big webs of skin for holding its position in the water while it rummages in the mud, as well as for powerful swimming.

A **seal's** arms and legs are both shaped like flippers or paddles. The seal swings its body from side to side, pushing with its rear flippers and steering with the front ones.

Inside some animals' flippers, legs, and wings the bones and joints are very similar to your arm. There's a shoulder, elbow, wrist, five fingers, and even small, nail-like claws on the fingertips.

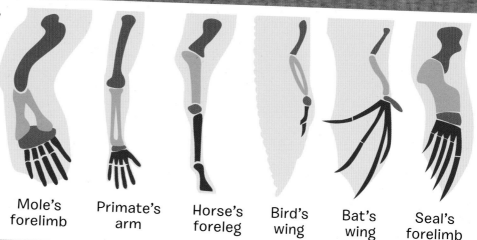

| Mole's forelimb | Primate's arm | Horse's foreleg | Bird's wing | Bat's wing | Seal's forelimb |

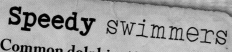

Speedy swimmers

Common dolphin 40 mph
Killer whale 31 mph
Fin whale 22 mph
Sea lion 15 mph
Human 5 mph

River dolphins

do not swim as far or as fast as their ocean cousins. So they have a smaller back fin and tail, and larger flippers more useful for making quick turns in small areas.

A dolphin has arm bones in its flippers, but no leg bones in its tail—its legs have disappeared as a result of evolution.

Home comforts

Human mammals like to share their lives with other creatures and many of these are also mammals. There are pet dogs, cats, and rabbits, to name a few. Other mammals such as cows, sheep, and pigs can be pets but mostly live on farms. Horses, donkeys, and camels are useful to humans and can be ridden. All of these animals are **domesticated mammals.**

Tasmanian devil

Devil of a pet

Sometimes people try to tame an unusual pet, like a sloth, raccoon, skunk, fox, wallaby, or even a Tasmanian devil. But they never become truly domesticated or safe.

The pet **cat** was one of the first domesticated animals. As much as 10,000 years ago, people recognized that with its sharp senses, it was useful for killing mice and rats around farms.

I couldn't be a pet. Where would my owner find 200 ants' nests every day?

Cows have been important to farmers for hundreds of years, both as dairy herds producing gallons of milk and as a supply of meat. Cows have a special four-part stomach. They chew and swallow grass and begin to digest it. Then they bring up lumps to chew again, called "chewing the cud," before swallowing and more digestion. This gets the most goodness out of their tough, low-nutrient food.

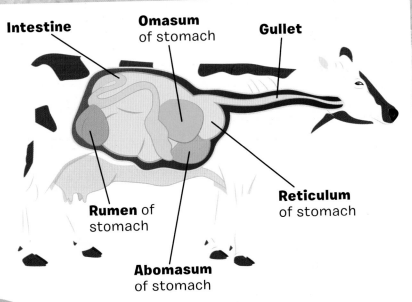

Intestine

Omasum of stomach

Gullet

Rumen of stomach

Reticulum of stomach

Abomasum of stomach

All mammal mothers make **milk** for their babies. Some domesticated mammals have been bred to make lots of milk for people—to drink, cook with, and make into cream, yogurt, and cheese. These include cows, goats, camels, sheep, horses, and yaks.

Farm animals vary around the world: **llamas** are common in South America, deer in Europe, camels in Africa, and water buffalo in Asia.

Llama

All at sea

Sea-living mammals have changed greatly from the usual land-dwelling kinds. They are sleek and streamlined, their arms are flippers—and some can hold their breath for hours!

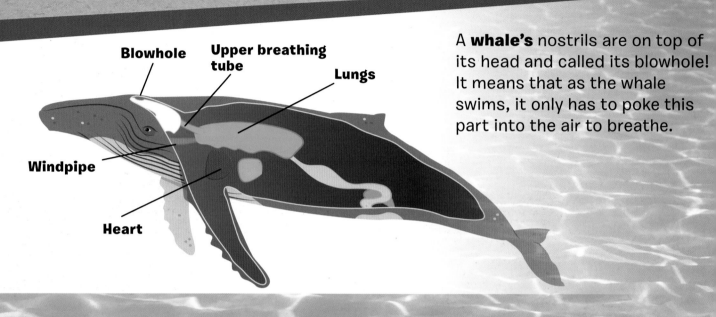

Blowhole

Upper breathing tube

Lungs

Windpipe

Heart

A **whale's** nostrils are on top of its head and called its blowhole! It means that as the whale swims, it only has to poke this part into the air to breathe.

Great whales have the world's biggest mouths, yet they eat shrimp-like krill, most of which are less than an inch long. Comb-like plates, called baleen plates, hang from the upper jaw. The whale gulps in water and food, closes its mouth, pushes the water out through the baleen, and licks up the krill trapped inside.

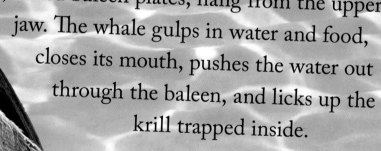

One kind of beaked whale dives down 2 miles, where it's always cold and totally dark!

Dolphins swim with others of their kind, in groups called pods or schools. They leap out of the water and splash back in, perhaps to send messages to each other—or just for fun!

Big breath-holders

Beaked whale 137 minutes
Elephant seal 120 minutes
Sperm whale 100 minutes
Dolphin 20 minutes
Sea otter 6 minutes
Human 22 minutes
(only after special training)

The **sea otter** prepares its food itself! It dives down to get a shellfish and a pebble from under the ocean. After popping back to the surface, it floats on its back and bashes the shell on its front with the pebble to get at the juicy animal inside. Other mammals use tools, too— see the next page.

Who's clever?

Mammals have big brains compared to their body size and are the cleverest creatures. They learn fast, remember for years, use tools, solve problems, and even invent games!

The brain is the body's control center. It receives information from the senses, makes decisions, stores memories, and controls movements. The **chimp** has one of the biggest brains for its body size.

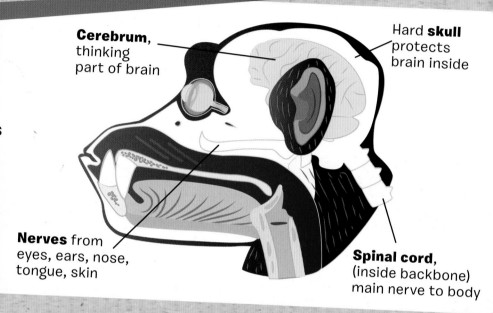

Cerebrum, thinking part of brain

Hard **skull** protects brain inside

Nerves from eyes, ears, nose, tongue, skin

Spinal cord, (inside backbone) main nerve to body

Chimps not only use tools, they actually make them by altering natural objects like twigs and stones, and even invent tools for new situations. This chimp is "fishing" in a termites' nest using a stem it has stripped of leaves.

My brain is quite small for my body—but it does the job!

Dolphins also use tools. They tear off bits of sponge and prod in the mud to find any hiding fish they can eat. The sponge is like a nose-glove and stops the dolphin's snout getting sore.

Elephants lick salty rocks to get minerals that keep them healthy. The herd leader, a female known as the matriarch, remembers where these special places are for more than 50 years.

Friends, enemies

Many mammals are **social**—they live in groups with their own kind. From giant herds of gazelles, antelopes, and zebras to small families of beavers, gorillas, and gibbons, they look after each other, feed in groups, and defend together against enemies.

The **beaver** family works to make their home—a dome of sticks, stones, and mud called a lodge. They build their lodges in streams, blocking the flow of water with more sticks and mud to create a dam with a little lake behind it.

Big families

Prairie dog town 50 million
(before reduction by humans)
Wildebeest herd 250,000
Caribou herd 150,000
Naked mole rat colony 75
African wild dog pack 15–25
Lion pride 10-20
Gorilla family 8–12
Beaver family 4–8
Human family 3–10

The shaggy-maned male **lion** roars to tell other lions' groups, called prides, to stay away from his own pride's area, or territory. The females' job is to hunt and kill animals like zebras and antelopes for the whole pride to eat.

Anteaters live mostly on their own. We like a quiet life!

Some mammals live mostly alone. The male **orangutan** sees a female only for a short time each year when breeding. Otherwise he keeps to himself through his lifetime of perhaps 40 or more years.

Baby time

Like all animals, mammals grow from **babies**, become adults, breed to make their own babies, get old, and die. This can take one year, or 200!

Usually male mammals are only slightly bigger and stronger than females. But sometimes the difference is enormous. The male **elephant seal** is as heavy as a real elephant at 4½ tons, yet the female weighs less than 1 ton.

As soon as a mammal is born, it must breathe air. That means a new baby **whale** or dolphin has to get to the surface quickly. The mother helps it to take its first gasps.

The babies of pouched mammals, or marsupials, like **kangaroos**, live at first in a pocket of skin on the mother's stomach. As they feed on her milk, they grow bigger and stronger, and start to explore outside.

Young **elephants** drink their mother's milk for up to three years, the longest of any mammal. The milk comes from parts called mammary glands which are located between the mother's front legs.

Longest recorded lives

Bowhead whale 200 years
Human 122 years
Elephant 86 years
Horse 62 years
Pet cat 38 years
Pet dog 29 years
Kangaroo 24 years
Mouse 4 years

I give my baby a piggyback. Or should that be anteater-back?

Glossary

beak: the stiff, pointed mouth structure of a bird for feeding, preening, and other tasks

blood: a liquid that travels all through the body, supplying oxygen and nutrients to all parts, and collecting wastes

bone: a hard material which makes up the skeleton of fish, amphibians, reptiles, birds, and mammals

brain: the part that receives information from the senses, makes decisions, and controls muscles

digest: to change food into simpler forms that can be taken in and used by the body

egg: a container for developing animals in their early stages

embryo: an animal in the early stages of growth before it is born

gill: the organ fish use to breathe underwater

graze: to eat grass and similar low plants

groom: to brush or clean the coat of an animal

gullet: the tube connecting an animal's mouth to its stomach

habitat: the natural home of an animal, like a pond, wood, or desert

heart: the part that pumps blood around the body

intestines: parts that take nutrients from digested food into the body

joint: the point where two parts, like bones, meet and usually can move

kidney: an organ that cleans the blood and makes a waste liquid, urine

liver: an organ that helps digest food, cleans the blood, and stores energy and nutrients

metamorphosis: major change to an animal's body structure, usually as part of becoming adult

muscles: parts that get shorter to pull and move the body

nerves: wire-like parts that carry messages between the brain and the body

nutrients: substances in food that animals need to live and grow

pectoral: a muscle in the upper body that moves the front limb, also the front side fin of a fish

pelvis: the lower back or base of the body, near the rear limbs, also the rear side fin of a fish

pincer: a type of claw with hinged parts that come together to hold, squeeze, and cut

predator: a creature that eats other creatures

scales: small, flat plates that form the outer covering of animals like fish and reptiles

shell: a tough, usually hard, protective outer covering, such as a snail shell, eggshell, or turtle shell

skeleton: the frame made up of bones that supports the body from the inside

stomach: where eaten food is stored and broken down as part of digestion

tentacle: a thin, bendy part used for moving about and grabbing, as in an anemone or octopus

venom: a harmful substance produced by some animals and jabbed in by bites, spines, and stings to hurt, paralyze, or kill other creatures

Index

Picture credits

Picture Researcher: Claire Gouldstone